SOUPS&STARTERS

STARTERS

SEAFOOD

SEAFOOD

MEAT

PASTA &RICE

PASTA

SALADS

SWEET
TREATS

SWEETS

10 9 8 7 6 5 4 3

Publishing Manager: Fiona Schultz
Designer: Tania Gomes
Production Controller: Linda Bottari
Printed in China

Cover photograph by Alamy
Internal images by R+R Publications PTY LTD

NEW HOLLAND PUBLISHERS

www.newholland.com.au